A Life With Anorexia

My Experience

I0103897

Jessica Mason

chipmunkapublishing

the mental health publisher

Published by

Chipmunkapublishing

PO Box 6872

Brentwood

Essex CM13 1ZT

United Kingdom

http://www.chipmunkapublishing.com

Edited by Aleks Lech

ISBN   978-1-84991-637-0

Chipmunkapublishing gratefully acknowledge the support of Arts Council England.

About The Author

Jessica Mason is 18 years old. She was born in 1992 and was close to dying as soon as her life started. She was born at 26 weeks.

Jessica now lives in Burgess Hill with her mum, twin sister and stepdad. Jessica doesn't see her dad anymore but is still in contact with him. He was very controlling as she grew up and didn't like her not doing what he wanted. He made Jessica feel guilty about the things she didn't do that he wanted her to do and blackmailed her into doing the things he wanted.

Jessica wrote the book "A life with Anorexia, My experience" because she wanted her story to be heard so it could help out other anorexic's and to show others what Anorexia can do to people.

Jessica is now working as a Nursery Practitioner at a local children's day Nursery. She got the job in 2009 and trained towards a NVQ level 2. Jessica is still controlled in some ways by her anorexia but is not classified as "ill". She was discharged from the mental health unit CAMHS in 2010 after nearly 2 whole years of going and receiving help.

She was diagnosed with Anorexia back in 2008 but feels she was showing signs of anorexia way before this year. She used to count calories in her head and enjoyed doing exercise until one day something changed.

Anorexia had a grip over her and told her what she should and shouldn't be doing and punished her for disobeying what it said. She lost loads of weight and suddenly had an intense fear of gaining weight and eating. She did everything she could to get out of eating.

All the secrecy lead her and her mum having arguments nearly every night and left Jessica feeling very depressed and suicidal . Once Jessica was prescribed with anti depressants in 2009 her life turned around and she started to get better.

This book is dedicated to my mum, step dad, grandma, granddad, twin sister, everyone at CAMHS, friends, and other family that have helped me through this difficult time in my life.

Contents

Chapter 1- About me

Chapter 2 -The old days

Chapter 3 - School's finished

Chapter 4 -Going to the doctors

Chapter 5 -The food Diary (that goes on till this day)

Chapter 6 -Being referred to CAMHS

Chapter 7 -In denial

Chapter 8- Stopping College and my life

Chapter 9 -Recovery

Chapter 10 -Finding my new life

Chapter 11- Holiday to Florida April 2010

Chapter 12 -My 18th Birthday

Chapter 13- Nearly recovered

Chapter 14 -The end

Chapter 1

About Me

Hi, my name is Jessica and I'm 18 years old. I was born at the Royal Sussex County Hospital in Brighton on 7th June 1992. I was born at 26 weeks. I was on oxygen for nearly a year and was close to dying before my life had even started.

I live at home with my mum, twin sister and step dad. I haven't lived in this house all my life; when I was a baby I lived in a house in Portslade. We then moved to a bigger house in Newhaven, then when my mum and dad split up (when I was aged ten) me, my sister and mum moved down the road to a smaller house, still in Newhaven. My mum then met a new boyfriend (who's now my stepdad) and they decided to move to Burgess Hill. We moved to Burgess Hill because all of my mum's family live in Burgess Hill or near Burgess Hill and my step dad's family also live in Burgess Hill. We also moved out here because we wanted a bigger house again.

My mum and dad split up when I was nine (January 2002). My dad told me and my sister that we were going to have two houses. He said that mum would be in the new one and that he would be in the family one. He also said that we were going to be living in the house with mum but we could go up and see him every weekend. He tried to make it sound exciting by saying that we would have two houses and that we would have two Christmases. We didn't fully understand what was actually happening I don't think because we didn't really seem upset at that time; we seemed to be more upset when we were looking around our new house and when our dad wasn't actually there. I will admit that I'm glad they split up because all I can remember from when I was younger was all the shouting and arguing they did, and I was always scared something bad would happen to one of them. I don't really remember spending time with my dad when I was younger because he was always working or doing other things.

My dad had met another woman (who's now my step mum) by the time we had moved out. She lived out in Switzerland, but soon moved over to England after my dad had been out to visit her a few times. I can remember the very first time that I met her. We went to see Monsters inc at the cinema. Dad picked me and my sister up from mum's house and we went off to the cinema, stopping off at the local McDonalds for dinner. I was really excited about going to the cinema and meeting her. Dad had told us so much about her that it made me really want to meet her. He had also told us loads of things about her past and about how the people out there were treating her horribly. This was only to make us feel sorry for her and to make us like her.

My dad was and still is very controlling. When I was ten after my mum and dad had split up they both came up with a rota for when we saw him. We didn't mind because we were too young really to make our own decisions so up until we were about twelve we used to see our dad every weekend. Friday night he would pick us up from mum's house, he would have us all day Saturday and then Sunday morning until 10am when mum would pick us up. Our dad would also have us Tuesday evenings when he picked us up at 6.00pm. When we got to twelve years we decided we didn't want to go there on Tuesdays because it was a bit pointless. By the time we got up there and put our things away we would be watching Eastenders and then going to bed so hardly saw him anyway. We also decided to go to his house every other weekend (Friday at 6.00, Saturday and Sunday until 6.00pm) so we could spend some weekends with our mum and go out with her too. During the week we stayed with mum.

By the time I was fifteen (year 10) I had decided I wanted to start doing what I wanted at weekends (instead of doing what he had planned) and meet friends, go out and basically have a life. This one time will stay in my mind forever. Me and my sister met our friend one Saturday; it was September time 2007, and we went to Brighton shopping for the day. We got the bus there and the bus back; dad had said he wanted us back by 4pm. At first we were like, can't we come back by at least 4.30 and he agreed with this, so off we went on the bus to Brighton. We had a fun day out and 4.30 came as quickly as a flash of light so we walked to the bus station to get on the next bus home. The bus happened to be delayed by 20 minutes (I think) so we stayed and waited for the bus and got on it. We thought we'd better text dad to let him know where we were. My sister texted him and said something along the lines of *"we're on the bus now, sorry we won't be home until about 5.40pm because the bus was delayed"*. We had no reply and when we got home we walked in and said "hi dad" and went up to him to show him what we had bought and he just completely ignored us so we walked away up to our rooms. A bit later he called us down and asked where we had gone and why we had walked away. I said "because you ignored us and didn't seem to want to look at our stuff". He then said something like "I didn't ignore you" and then started shouting that we were late and that we didn't tell him where we were and that he was scared, so we said that we did text him to say what was happening and he was like "well you should have rung so I could have spoken to you." When we got home and told mum about this she was very angry with him and we then both decided we didn't want to see him again until further notice because he was so controlling and didn't let us do the things we wanted. He didn't like us doing things when we wanted to but he always tried to get us to make new friends and go out to after school clubs when he wanted us to. He used to say that we had come to see him so we should stay with him and be with him.

I also remember this time when he had booked a trampoline club for me and my sister to go to for one Saturday at the local leisure centre. We both didn't want to go because we didn't like going to clubs and found it hard to socialise anyway without this added pressure. We were talking about it all night and were trying to figure out a way of getting out of going but couldn't. The next morning came so off we went. When we got to the leisure centre we were both waiting outside the doors for ages deciding whether to go in or not. (We were thinking of looking around the town instead and then pretending that we had been when dad asked about it.) By the time we walked in we had missed the first half an hour and the instructor was surprised that we came in because there wasn't a lot of time left for the trampolining. When we got back to dad's house he asked us how it was and whether we had made any new friends and we said we didn't really enjoy it and didn't want to go again.

Since the 2007 shopping experience I haven't seen my dad at a weekend again like the old times. I have still stayed in contact with him though, well have tried to anyway. He's the one who hasn't made the effort really. Each year on his birthday I text him to say happy birthday and I would ask him what he had done and whether he had had a good day. He would reply, "not really because I didn't see you, nothing, just been sitting around crying." It was really upsetting for me to read these sorts of messages because they were really sad and it made me feel guilty about not seeing him. I had to stay strong though. I knew I couldn't go running back into his arms because I knew he would just do the same thing again soon after. He sent me a birthday text on my 17th birthday (I think) at around 8pm though, so he couldn't even have been bothered to send me a text throughout the day. I was beginning to think that he wasn't going to bother. Even my step mum had sent me a birthday text before him; she sent me one on the morning of my birthday. I never received presents from them either, nor my grandma and grandpa (dad's mum and dad). They all said that my presents were waiting at his house for when I went there. They were clearly trying to get me there but this wasn't the way to go about it. They were all as bad as each other. Dad was very childish. I used to receive loads of texts from him that would say things like "when are you coming to see me, why are you doing this to me? What have I done to deserve this?, ???????? Do you love me? You're breaking my heart". He used to say other things like if you come and see me you can have this or that etc. etc. This was basically to get us to go there and of course it worked for a while because I wanted the things he was offering. I did arrange to see my dad in June time 2009 and he did meet me. This was a very nervous time because I hadn't seen him properly for almost two years and I knew what he was like. I knew he would ask lots of questions like why hadn't I seen him, what had he done to stop me from seeing him, even though he knew why and what he'd done, he just couldn't accept it and didn't believe he was being controlling.

I now haven't heard from my dad since March/April time 2010. I have sent him a Christmas card this year (like I have done every year). I wonder what I'll get in return. I also started writing to my grandma and grandpa with just general chit chat to see how they are. They have started replying properly and nicely and haven't been saying much about dad and how upset he is which is good. I have also received a few of my past birthday and Christmas presents from my grandma which was very thoughtful of them and I'm very grateful. Dad wasn't ever physically abusive; he was just emotionally abusive and used emotional blackmail.

There are a load more memorable experiences that I can remember but I won't talk any more about this subject.

Chapter 2

Old Days

When I was little I never ever even thought about food and what I ate or how much I should have to eat. I was just a normal girl that did normal things. I have never really been a fan of food from what I remember but still, I was all right with eating food. I used to love going out to eat, especially at night time because I used to love coming home in the dark. I never used to think about what I could eat and what I couldn't eat, I used to get to the pub and eat whatever I wanted, and a lot of the time I would have pudding too.

In my opinion i was quite chubby when I was nine, ten and eleven years old but everyone just said it was puppy fat so I thought it would disappear when i got older. I do remember it disappearing but I don't know whether that was because I got older or whether it was from what I ate. In year 7 (aged eleven) I carried on eating the same things for lunch as I had been eating from when I was younger. This used to include a sandwich (two slices of bread) with a filling (such as turkey slices, tuna, cheese), a piece of fruit, a yoghurt, a cheese string and a cake. When I got to around 11 ½ years I changed my lunch completely and used to just eat a salad and a piece of fruit. The salad contained some lettuce (probably 30g), a tomato, a chunk of cucumber, some packet turkey (10 slices roughly), and some cheese (about 35g). I didn't change this for any reason to help me lose weight, I changed to something smaller because it used to take me most of my lunch break to eat it and I didn't want to always be the last one eating. This meant that by the time I was twelve/thirteen years I was slimmer. I liked it, obviously, because everyone likes to lose weight, but I wasn't trying to lose weight. I used to eat sweets when we were given them at school and I used to just eat what I wanted. I sometimes bought food at the end of school in the town. I never did any additional exercise either, all the exercise I did was walking to and from school and to and from the train station, and twice a week when I would do a PE lesson which would only last ½ hour by the time everyone was changed and ready. By year 10 I didn't do any PE lessons because I didn't choose to do PE as one of my options.

When I was fourteen (year 9) I did go through a phase of watching what I ate more than before and I did like to count calories. I didn't count them properly though, (like I didn't look on each thing I ate and add it up) I just guessed roughly how much I was eating in a day. It was working out that I was eating around 1500 a day which I liked because it meant I wouldn't gain weight. I think I went through this stage because I was watching quite a few programmes on slimming and how much people should eat in a day. I was also watching programmes with overweight people trying to lose weight so I was trying to follow in some of their footsteps. I didn't actually take it too seriously though, luckily. The funny thing was though, I stayed the same weight right from when I was thirteen all the way till I was sixteen, when I first got ill.

I remember our family holiday to the peak district when I was fourteen years old in August 2006. I had lost all my puppy fat and I really liked my looks. I think I looked really slim and my skin looked tight around my face. I couldn't actually pinch much skin so I knew I wasn't fat and I liked it. I knew I didn't want to put on weight and did watch what I ate, but never to the extreme. We went swimming whilst on holiday and I actually wore a bikini which I would never do now and never did like to do when I was younger. We went out for dinner twice in a week and I didn't think anything of it and enjoyed the holiday. I had a proper meal and a pudding with both the meals out. For breakfast I had croissants and chocolate spread and for lunch I had a sandwich, fruit and two cakes, so this was a proper amount of food. While on the holiday I did faint when we went swimming (but this was most probably because we had lunch at 2.30 and had had breakfast early in the morning ready for swimming so it was too long without food). We then came back to our cottage and I had a chocolate bar. I wouldn't have had that when I was ill. We also hired some bikes and went on a thirteen mile bike ride around all the downs and parks which I really did enjoy. This was only because I enjoyed exercising, not because I felt I had to do it.

In 2007 there was a programme on about anorexics and I watched it because it looked good. I never thought I would be like that a few years later and I didn't really understand what it was and how those people could live like it. I felt really sorry for all the girls on that programme and hoped they would get better soon.

Chapter 3

School's Finished

My last day at Lewes Priory School was supposed to be May 16th 2008, but then it got brought forward to May 14th due to exams on May 16th and the 15th.

After school was finished I made sure I did revision for all my upcoming GCSE's. I used to spend most of the day revising and would have a couple of hours break. I really wanted to do well in my exams, so I knew I had to revise for them. In my breaks I had started to exercise. This made me feel in control of my body and I felt happy with myself for doing the exercise. By doing this it helped me to feel less fat and lazy for sitting around all day revising. I then set a target in my head; for every break I had I had to do exercise. I did make sure though that I ate a proper amount to help me concentrate on revision and so I didn't get distracted easily.

My first exam was in May and my last exam was in June so I was really lucky that all my exams were all in one big block instead of being spread out along the whole summer.

Once all my exams had finished I decided I still needed to do my hours exercise each day, so I started going out on the trampoline and on the wii fit. To start off with I only did up to two hours. Then it started to get worse. I used to spend most of the day on the wii fit. I would try to see if I could do more and more minutes on there each day and see if I could beat what I had already done the day before. I still didn't feel as if anything was that bad though, and just thought this was better than sitting around doing nothing all day.

On June 25 2008 it was my school prom. It was held in Alfriston and I was really looking forward to it. I wasn't worried about the food and eating, I was just generally excited about going. I travelled there and back in a limo with my sister and a friend. My grandma made my dress for me. It was pink with horizontal white frills going all the way down it. I really liked it and was very grateful to my grandma for making it for me. I was meant to have my hair curled and have some hair extensions put in but my hairdresser couldn't make it on the day because of other circumstances so in the end I had my hair down and straightened. It wasn't the best hair do but there was nothing else I could do. The school prom lasted about four hours and we left at about 11.30pm.

It was after the school prom that I started exercising more and more and eating less. I stopped going on the wii fit and started using the trampoline because I had heard and read that trampolining is the best exercise to do because you use every muscle, so once I had seen this I thought I'd try it and see if I lost weight. At this point I did actually want to lose a bit of weight, I don't really know why, I just did. My day to day routine would be, get up at 8.00am, go downstairs and get the rabbits out into their run, and go on the trampoline until about 10.00am. Then I would go back upstairs so that my sister didn't know I had already done two hours exercise. I would then have breakfast with her. I had started having Special K for breakfast because I knew it was low in calories and good for me. I didn't weigh it out exactly, I just put a small amount in the bowl. Then my sister would go upstairs on her laptop and I would get dressed and go back out on the trampoline. I was out on it for the whole morning until my sister came down for some lunch. I would then go inside for some lunch with her. I had started eating salads again but I would have less of the turkey and cheese. I even made my mum buy the smaller packet of turkey because I wasn't eating it all and it was being wasted. This was a good excuse also for me to have less because the packet had to last me the week. I didn't have anything else for lunch. Then I would go back out on the trampoline until about 3.30pm when my mum came home. Sometimes I would go back out there while mum made the dinner. At dinner times I made sure I ate less than normal too. A lot of the time I skipped puddings and just said I was full, or I would do the washing up and just go straight upstairs to watch Eastenders afterwards. No one suspected a thing, so I was getting away with it which was what I liked. Each day I would make sure I ate the same or less. I made up my own calorie allowance in my head and would count up roughly how much I was eating. I made sure I didn't eat more than 1500 calories in a day. This was also because you lose a pound a week by eating 500 calories less than an average person should eat, so I had got that in my head and I was hoping I would lose even more weight because of the amount of exercise I was doing together with the lack of food I was eating. As this became a more obsessive thing I hated not doing any exercise. If I didn't do any exercise I would punish myself by exercising in my room at night when everyone had gone to bed. By the time it got to August I had lost weight and I was weighing myself over ten times a day. I would weigh myself every time I went into the bathroom. I really liked myself and I started to hear voices in my head saying horrible things to me like "I'm fat, I need to lose weight" and "I'm doing well" and to "keep going".

My holiday in August 2008 was to Wells and Bath. I was quite excited about this holiday, apart from the fact that I knew I would have to go a whole week without any intense exercise and I wouldn't have control over my weight. I tried to make my head believe that it would be OK and that I wouldn't have to eat loads to make up for not exercising. On the way to our cottage we stopped off at my auntie's house for some lunch. I only had half a sandwich, I can't remember what I had in it, and one small home made cake that she had made. We then played on the wii (not the wii fit) for a bit and then set off again in the car. On this holiday we visited lots of different places including cheddar gorge, the Roman baths, the zoo and the beach. We took our lunch with us every day as a picnic. The first few days I took a sandwich, a piece of fruit and one cake, then I started taking less and wouldn't even eat it all. This made me feel better about doing no exercise so I felt happy. Mum didn't say anything to me about why I wasn't finishing my food so I didn't think she noticed. It was when we got home and once I got back into my exercising routine that she called me aside and asked me why I was exercising so much. I said that I wasn't doing a lot and that it was fun. She then said "You're not trying to lose weight are you?" so I quickly said "No, of course not". Deep down I knew I was. I hated lying to my mum, it was horrible but I knew if I said yes to that question she would stop me going on the trampoline and I would hate that, so I thought the best option was to lie.

I still didn't think I was ill but I knew that there was something inside of me that was stopping me from eating certain things and something that was making me do all this exercise, but I didn't want to find out what it was because I liked the control it had over me. I didn't think anything would ever get to a dangerous level.

Chapter 4

Going To The Doctors

In September 2008 mum said to me that she was taking me to the doctors. I wasn't too sure why, but didn't really ask why either. So off we went to the doctors. When I was at the doctors all they did was weigh me and asked me a few questions about what I eat on a normal day to day basis. She didn't seem too concerned so I was lucky. She said she wanted to see me again in two weeks time so I could be weighed again so they could keep track of my weight. Two weeks came by and I was off to the doctors again, where I got weighed again. I had lost more weight. I now weighed 37kg. I then saw the doctor another two times where she weighed me. Each time I had lost weight. I was so happy with myself. She said she wanted me to write a food diary so she could see everything I ate each week. I did this and took it with me on the next appointment. When I showed her my food plan she said that it seemed to be an OK amount of food but clearly it wasn't because I kept losing more and more weight.

At this point I was still exercising loads each day, not so much on the trampoline though because I had started college and didn't have as much time, but I was jogging in my room each night. I would stay awake till midnight and sometimes past midnight exercising.

I got down to 36.5kg and my doctor said she was getting worried about my weight and thought that she was going to refer me to a unit to get help. As soon as she said this I got really scared because I knew this would be the end of my control. She referred me to CAMHS.

She explained to me that she thought I was anorexic and she asked me what I thought when she said the word anorexic. I just said "It's scary but I can't stop exercising."

I was still allowed to exercise though which I was pleased about. The doctor didn't know about my secret exercising that I was doing and neither did mum. By now my periods had stopped too. They didn't come back properly until September time 2009. My periods now are not regular (every 4 weeks) but I do get them most months which means I'm healthy which is good.

In November 2008 we went ice-skating with my cousins and their parents. I don't remember much from it, but what I do remember is that I was only excited about going ice-skating because of the hour-long exercise. I went round the rink a lot and tried to do loads of exercise because I knew that that would be the only amount of exercise I would be allowed to do that day. I didn't talk to my cousins hardly at all and just isolated myself. We stopped and had some food when we had finished the ice-skating. The only choice of food that was available was fast food. I was so worried. I didn't know what to have and the person in my head was saying things like "Don't eat this shit, you'll get even fatter than you already are" and was trying to get me out of eating it. My mum then agreed with me that I could have a children's meal so I chose plain chicken with chips from KFC. I really couldn't eat this and was so scared about each mouthful. Everyone had finished and I had hardly started which made me feel even worse because it felt as if everyone was watching me eat. I didn't like this thought at all and my head was hurting from it, saying don't eat and things like that so I quickly hid some of the chicken under the food bag it came in and didn't manage all the chips because I found a hair in them which totally put me off. I then said I had finished and threw it away quickly so no one could come to check whether I had hidden anything.

By this time mum was still allowing me to do exercise, but just not too much of it each day. She allowed me to do around 30-60 minutes. I was happy with this because I knew I could do my secret exercise that no one knew about. She was starting to get worried about me and my weight by this time as well, but I just couldn't see what the big problem was. Mum knew that I was weighing myself loads in a day so she hid the scales. When I went into the bathroom to weigh myself I was shocked when the scales had gone. I didn't know where they were and I was getting worried in case mum secretly knew about the other things I was doing like the secret exercise or the hiding of the food. This also made me feel way out of control because I now had no idea what I weighed until weigh day at CAMHS. All my head was saying to me was that I should have put the scales back properly and that I shouldn't have weighed myself until everyone was downstairs. It was too late though. I was starting to lose all control and my anorexic self didn't like it.

Chapter 5

The Food Diary (that still goes on to this day)

The food diary; where do I start with this? I started writing out what I ate each day after I visited the doctors in 2008. I still didn't attempt to eat any extra; even though I knew I was being referred to CAMHS, I was just too scared to eat. I was still weighing myself so many times each day until mum took away the scales which was right up until about November/December 2008. The next couple of pages are pictures of my food plans when I was in control, the diet I was made to eat once I was referred to CAMHS and also the sorts of things I eat nowadays whilst trying to maintain my weight. When I was writing down what I was eating in a day I was only managing to reach up to 1000 calories a day. Once I had been referred to CAMHS my mum had to take control of my food and food plans and I was made to eat 2500 calories by being force fed by mum. I had to eat three snacks a day with a big breakfast, lunch and dinner to be able to get up to 2500 calories. Now that I'm almost better and am eating properly I only have to eat between 1600 – 2000 calories depending on my weight and how much weight I put on each week etc.

I think the reason I still like my mum to write out my food plans is because she has done it since Christmas 2008. I still don't mind about eating too few calories which shows that I'm still getting anorexic thoughts which I personally don't think will ever disappear out of my life.

I was basically a walking skeleton by the time mum took control. Everyone would say that I was TOO thin but I just couldn't see it and didn't believe it. Everyone was always telling me to just eat but it's not that easy. My hair was also falling out but I still couldn't seem to see what was happening to me. No one will ever fully understand this and how anorexia works unless they have or are experiencing this illness.

These few food lists are when I was in control.

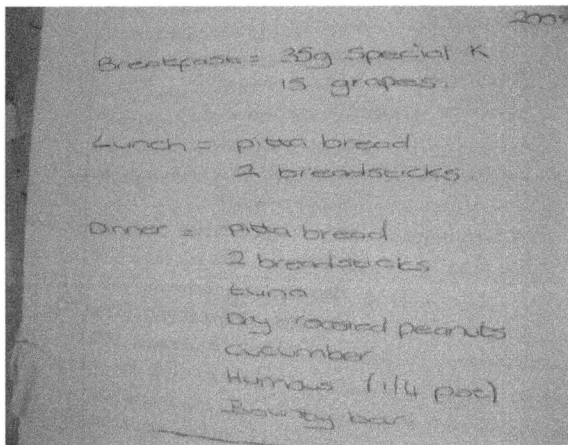

The bread sticks were mini ones, the pitta bread was normal size, the bounty bar was a mini sized one.

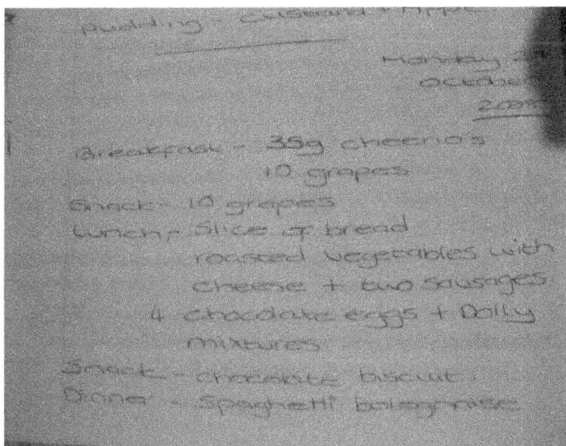

The chocolate eggs were mini ones, the dinner was a small portion.

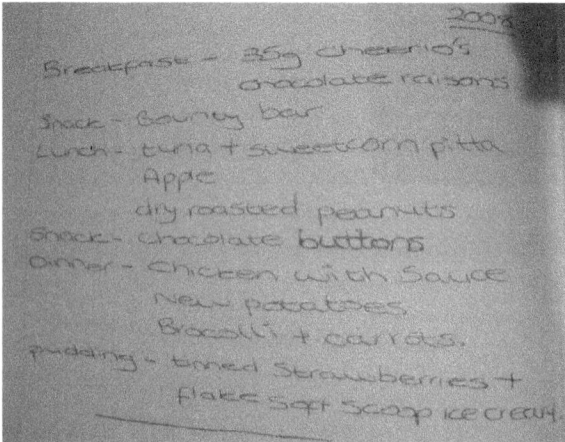

The bounty bar was a mini snack size (fun size), chocolate buttons were only a mini pack (fun size), ice cream was one scoop or less, tinned fruit was less than ½ pack.

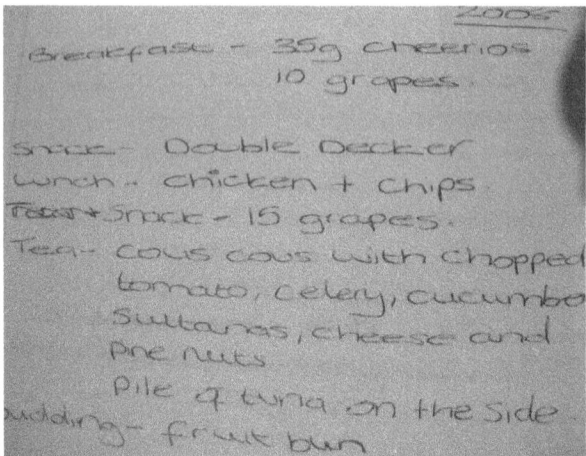

The double decker was a big normal size one. I didn't eat it all though. The chicken and chips were the KFC meal that I didn't manage (this was the day of the ice skating).

This was when mum started to get a bit more worried about me and she made me add up what I was eating in a day so I could see that I wasn't over eating. I was still in control over what I ate. The chocolate bar here was a fun size dairy milk.

The porridge here was only a small sachet of Winnie the Pooh children's porridge which I made with water, not milk, chocolate buttons again were a fun size packet and the chocolate was another fun size dairy milk.

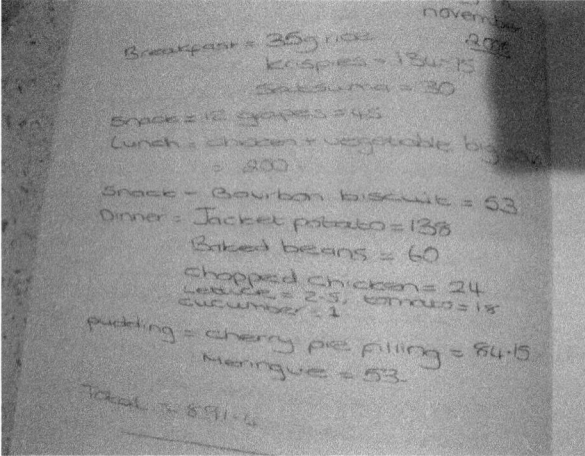

As you can see I was eating less and less. I was feeling good about myself. These next few are when mum took charge. The next picture shows the amount of calories mum was getting me to eat on those days.

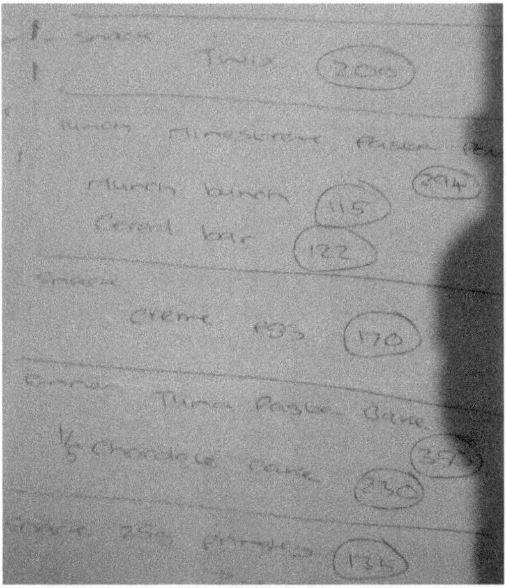
Snack
Twix 200
lunch Minestrone
294
Munch bunch 115
Cereal bar 122
Snack
creme egg 170
Dinner Tuna Pasta Bake
1/5 Chocolate cake 230
Snack 25g Pringles 135

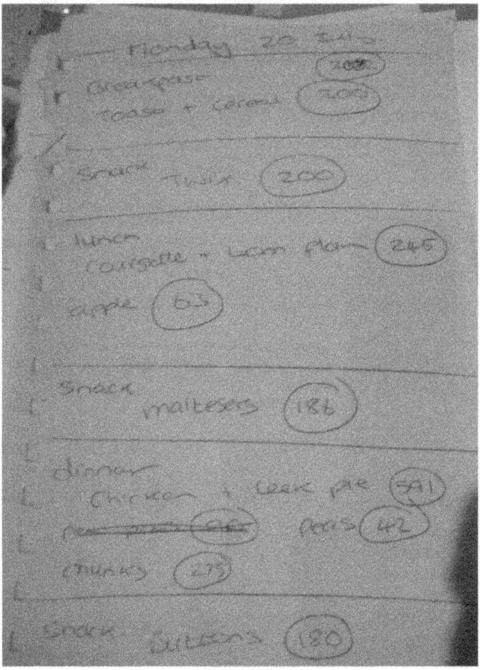
Monday 20 July
Breakfast
Toast + cereal 300
Snack Twix 200
lunch
courgette 245
apple 63
Snack
maltesers 186
dinner
chicken + leek pie 591
peas 42
Snack buttons 180

As you can see mum wrote down the amount and the calories I was having each day so she knew exactly what I was eating. I wasn't allowed to see this book because mum didn't want me to know how much I was eating.

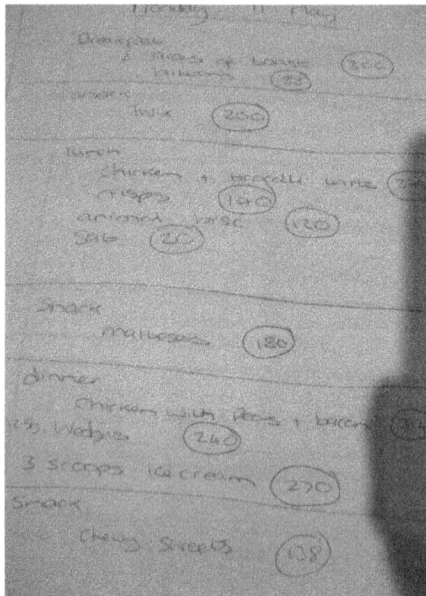

This is the sort of things I eat nowadays. I tend to stick between 1500-1900 depending on my weight.

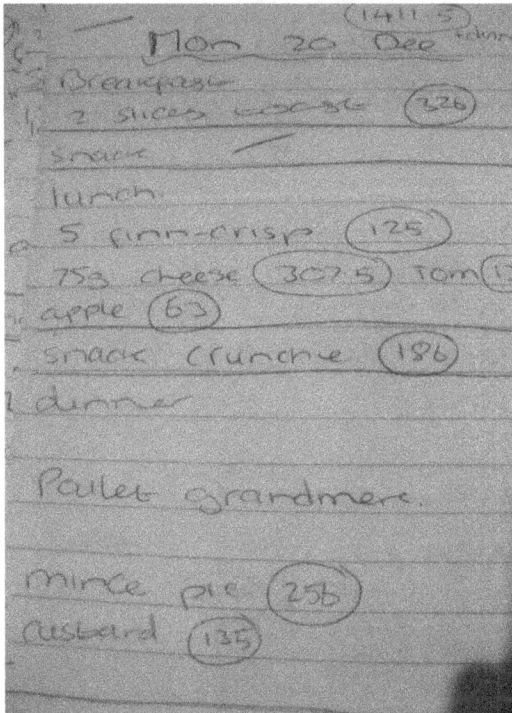

This is the size of the book which has every meal plan in it from right back to when I was writing down what I was eating when the doctor told me to.

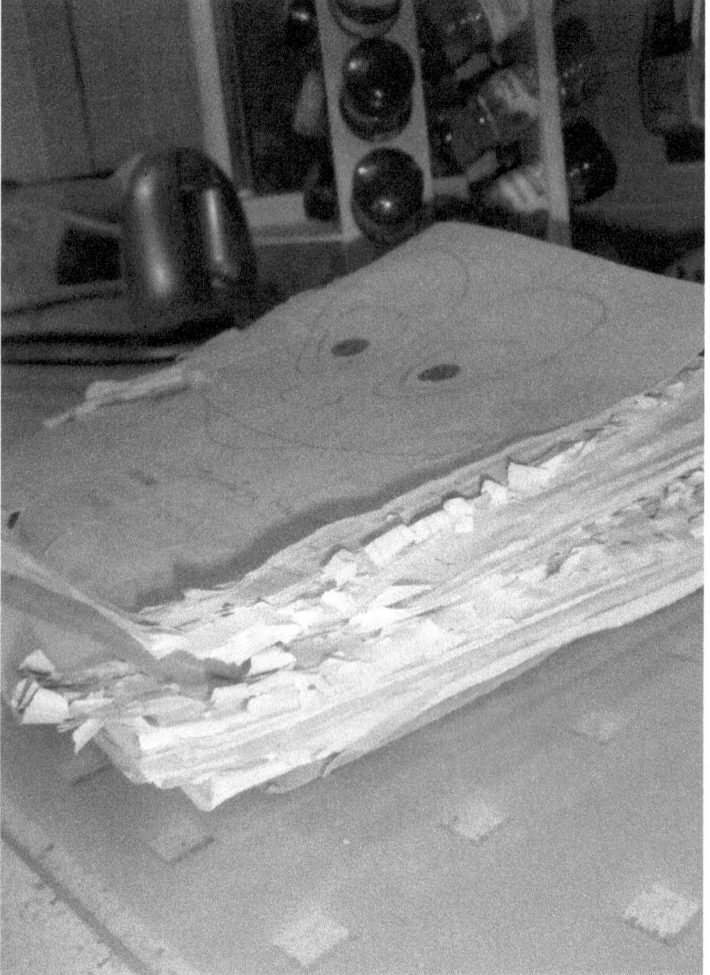

Chapter 6

Being Referred To CAMHS

Well, i got referred to CAMHS which stands for Child's adolescent mental health services back in November time by the doctor. My first appointment was the middle of November 2008, with Emily. The first meeting was where my mum and I got to know everyone in the team and Emily got to know me a little. She was talking to me about anorexia and what I liked about it. She got me to choose a picture of what I felt I looked like and I had the time to talk to her on my own about how I was feeling, and my own worries and problems. She also weighed me and noted it down so the team could keep a record of my weight. She said that I needed to start putting on weight as I'd be in hospital or I would maybe die but I just didn't believe her and didn't want to believe her because I didn't believe I was thin and I wanted to be thinner.

The next appointment I went to was only a week or so later where I got to meet up with Emily again and also the doctor, David the psychiatrist. They both spoke to me about my feelings and what would happen if I kept loosing weight. They said I would end up in hospital and that they would refer me to the hospital if need be. David also said that if I lost more weight I would die. I didn't take this seriously because Emily had said that the week before and I was still there, alive, after having lost even more weight. They were trying to scare me but it didn't work. Nothing worked because I still didn't believe anything anyone was saying. Everyone saying I was ill and too thin and stuff but I couldn't believe them. Anorexia wouldn't allow me to listen to anyone apart from it. They said their goodbyes and said that my next appointment would be with a specialist mental health nurse and she would work with me to help me get better. (No one had stopped me from exercising still so I was still exercising on the trampoline for a little bit most days after college. I was also still doing my jogging that no one knew about)

So the next appointment was with Kirsti, the mental health nurse. I went with my grandma because my mum was starting her new job that day so she couldn't come with me. I went in the room on my own and she spoke to me about how I felt and why I was feeling this way. She listened to me while I spoke and didn't interrupt or anything. It was really nice to get it all out in the open but also on the other hand I didn't want her to know everything because I was already scared about losing control over my life by even going to CAMHS in the first place, so I made sure I didn't tell her the truth about everything. She weighed me and took my blood pressure and said she was really worried and concerned about me and said that I would die if I lost any more weight. By this time my weight had plummeted to 35.4 kg/ 5st 5lb and my blood pressure was so low that I was awaiting a heart attack. She said that i couldn't lose any more weight. I defiantly didn't believe her because the week before David had said the exact same thing and yet again I hadn't died. I was still alive and didn't feel anything. No pain and no emotions; I really liked it that way, having no worries at all. She then came up with a solution for me to stop losing weight and that was to go into hospital and to stop college altogether. As soon as I heard what she said I was panicking like mad because I really didn't want to go into hospital because I had heard things about the hospitals that i didn't like and that I knew my anorexia just wouldn't like. The things I had heard were that you have to eat what they give you or you get tube fed, you can't do anything, they watch you 24/7. I was also scared my mum would be angry with me and that everyone who had tried helping me would be angry and disappointed with me.

Kirsti called grandma into the room and told her what was going to be happening. My grandma straight away said "No, she can live with me and I'll look after in the house instead of her going into hospital". Kirsti agreed that this was an OK decision but said that if I didn't listen to grandma and granddad I would go straight to hospital. I agreed to this and straight away all my mind was thinking about was how do I get out of eating and planning what my next bit of food would be. We made another appointment for a week's time and Kirsti gave me some instructions that I had to follow. They included, eat 2500 calories a day, wear loads of layers so I don't get cold and have a duvet over me at all times, drink lots of water, don't do anything, sit in the chair the whole day. My food was now not controlled by me, it was controlled by my mum. I was very scared. Kirsti had said to grandma that I could eat as much chocolate as I needed to to get me up to eating 2500 a day. I had no dietician to help mum with my meal plans either, so I had to eat loads of unhealthy foods to get my weight up. This was also a worry for me because I didn't think this was safe.

Once grandma and I were in the car we drove into town so I could choose some lunch for me to have for that day. I needed something much higher in calories than what I had packed for lunch already. I was wondering around Waitrose trying to pick out something, but I was finding it so hard to choose because I felt everyone was watching and looking at me. I couldn't help but look at the calories in everything I picked up and I was trying to move around the most I could to burn up extra calories. I finally found the soups and thought I'd get one of them. I chose the smallest calorie one first, thinking grandma wouldn't look, that's how deceiving and nasty I was, but she did look and said that wasn't enough. The thoughts that were going around my head were making me really angry with myself and I couldn't concentrate properly. I eventually found a soup and we left to go back to my grandma's house.

When I arrived at grandmas, granddad was standing there looking puzzled. Grandma told him to go into the lounge so I could tell him what was happening. I went and sat down on the sofa and told him what was happening, but the thing was I still didn't believe it and I felt weird when I was telling him. I said that I would be living with them every day until I was better and that my weight had got down to a dangerous level and that I wasn't allowed to do anything at all. I said that I had another meeting with Kirsti next week and I would find out then whether I would be taken to hospital.

All my clothes were too big by this time and I still couldn't see the difference. Before this day I was hardly eating anything, but no one knew that I wasn't eating it all because I was throwing away my lunch in the bins around college. I did this very secretly; I would go to the toilet every lunch time and throw away the unwanted food in the sanitary bins. I was very deceitful and really thought I was doing well. One time when I was on the train coming home from college I still had my lunch in my bag because I hadn't had time to go to the toilet so I went to the toilet on the train. My sister said I had to leave my bag with her, but I quickly made up an excuse that I needed my bag with me. This really panicked me because I thought she had an idea of what I was doing. I felt so happy after I'd thrown the food away because I knew then that I had got away with it once again. Mum had started searching through my college bag each night before I took it upstairs to check I had eaten my lunch, she would always ask me whether I'd eaten it all and I would say yes. I knew if I said no she would make me eat more food later and I would be really worried about that because I then wouldn't have any idea with how many calories I had eaten that day. Every time mum found me hiding food or exercising she would make me eat more food to make up the difference. Anorexia hated this obviously and always made me do loads of exercise to burn it off.

Chapter 7

In Denial

Basically throughout the whole time I started this exercise regime and the trying to lose weight thing I was in denial. I just didn't believe I was thin, I didn't believe anything anyone said to me and I didn't want to believe it. I don't know why I didn't want to believe it but I knew I didn't want to live any more and didn't want to get better. I knew once I put on the weight that CAMHS wanted me to put on I would be more tempted to lose it again. No one seemed to understand this and no one knew what it was like to be in my shoes and it really annoyed me when everyone said I needed to get better and that they knew what I was going through because they didn't have a clue.

At Christmas 2008 I joined this site called BEAT which was where lots of other girls talked about how they felt and what they were going through themselves. I didn't go on it much to start with, but was soon on it most nights. I was posting lots of comments on how I didn't want to live and how I wanted my family to stop going on at me. I really liked having other people to talk to that actually knew what I was going through because it just made it feel so much easier to talk about it all. It made me feel like I wasn't the only one going through it and that I could get over the illness one day. You could post messages about yourself and how you felt, and there was a section for people who had someone in their life who was ill and they could write down what they were going through and they got advice on how to help them get through it.

I drafted an email that I was going to send to my mum about how I felt because I couldn't face talking to her face to face about it. This is what it said

Hey

I'm sorry for being annoying about food. I don't mean to. Every time I have a good day of eating I just feel bad and that's why I muck around... I'm just scared ... I don't want to go to hospital but I'm just scared about putting on weight too. I'm not doing it on purpose... WELL I suppose I am in a way cos I know that I'm doing it but I can't help it...
I don't like having these arguments and I just want to be happy.
I don't know why I'm doing it... I suppose it's cos I want to lose weight and I'm scared of putting on weight... I need to get all that out of my head and once it's gone hopefully I will be able to get better but I don't see how it's gonna get out of my head cos once I have put on weight I'm just gonna want to lose it again.........

I never sent this because I felt bad about what I was saying. I didn't want to upset my mum and I didn't want her to know how I was feeling either because I still wanted that bit of control over my life. I drafted this in November 2008.

I also started talking to my auntie about what was going on in my life. I wanted to have someone to talk to, I didn't want them to help me though still, I think, I was hoping for them to suggest what I could do to lose weight. I have no idea why I was thinking this because it's obvious now that anyone who loves you and cares for you isn't going to help you lose weight, they would only help you get better.

The email I sent to my aunty said:

I'm having a lot of trouble with eating at the moment... I'm off college at the moment because I'm not allowed to get too cold. I just have to rest all the time. Its sooo hard.

I'm really scared because if I lose any more weight I will go into hospital. I'm going back to CAMHS on Tuesday so that's when I will find out.

Do you have any advice that might help me?

We're putting our decorations up this weekend so that should be fun...

Love you xxxxxx

She replied with this....

Hi Jess,

Good to hear from you. Sorry you are not doing so great at the moment. I am not an expert on this at all but was so happy you felt you could talk to me about it. I have been thinking about you loads. What do you think led you to this point in your life? Have CAMHS been helpful in helping you understand what is happening to you? I hope so. You are a wonderful person and you do not deserve this to be happening to you. Sorry I haven't been much help but I am always here for you and will always listen to you.

Stay in touch,

Love you lots,

Mandy xx

This brings tears to my eyes reading both these emails because I didn't believe I was ill and I just don't see how I got down to this point in my life. I still don't know what triggered it and won't ever know. It's just sad to think my life could have ended that year by me dying; just how would my family have coped? I can't believe I did this to myself and my family. What was I thinking?

Me and my mum had so many arguments over my illness. She used to say things like I would go into a mental home if I didn't eat, and if I wanted my hair to fall out then I should carry on with what I was doing to myself. I always got confused when she said this and would always say back , but I'm not mental. She didn't mean this horribly, she just couldn't cope with what was happening. I can't believe we actually got through it and I can't believe we still have the old bond we used to have when I was younger. It's like nothing ever happened.

I didn't believe that I would die because people had said that to me lots of times and I never did die. I was in denial right up until I was up to my target weight. I'm still a little in denial now about the illness, like I sometimes don't believe I was ever ill. I think this is because I hear all these stories from other girls who suffer from anorexia who go into hospital and who actually die so this just makes me feel that I was a joke and a fake but what I have to keep reminding myself is that I wouldn't have been referred to CAMHS if I wasn't ill and I wouldn't have been given the help if I wasn't ill.

Chapter 8

Stopping College and My Life

As you now know I was signed off college at the beginning of December 2008 and was living at my grandma's. This was definitely no fun at all and I hated it. Each morning I would get up early at 6.30am, go downstairs, wait for mum to go to work and for my grandma to arrive. I had to get up at this time so mum knew I was up and not doing anything I shouldn't have been doing. Grandma would arrive at about 7.30 just as my mum was leaving for work and she would make me my breakfast. I hated anyone else making my breakfast because I knew it would be exactly right and I would just hate myself so much for eating it. I had no control over my food and weight by this time and I did not like it. I would stand upstairs for ages naked just staring at myself in the mirror and I would hope that all the fat would disappear. I was so adamant that I wanted the fat to go that I would exercise in my room in the mornings after breakfast. My breakfast would be made by 8.00am and it would take me at least half an hour just to eat it, and then to top that off I would sit at the dinner table thinking about what I had just eaten, what I was doing to myself and listening to the voices in my head for another half an hour. I would then get up and go and get dressed. It didn't take me long to choose my clothes because I only had about two sets of clothes that I used to wear because nothing else fitted. I didn't care what I looked like so it didn't matter to me that I had no other clothes to choose from. I was now into children's jeans size 9/10. I would turn on the radio and time half an hour on my clock for me to do my exercise. It made me feel good doing this exercise because I knew I wouldn't get another chance to do it and most of all I knew I wasn't allowed to do it so it made me feel even better. I couldn't live with myself if I didn't do any exercise; at least if I did a little bit my mind wouldn't be so bad and I wouldn't feel as bad about my looks. It sounds like I was just doing it because I knew I wasn't allowed to. It wasn't like that, it was that I felt good about doing the exercise because I knew then I wasn't eating all the calories that had been worked out for me to have so then I thought I wouldn't put on any weight if that makes sense. I was basically kidding myself about what I was doing. I think I also found it so hard because I knew everyone was trying to get me to put weight on so I knew if I did what I was meant to do then I would put on the weight and I really didn't want to. I was still in denial.

After I had done my half an hour jogging I would finally get dressed and come downstairs so we could go to grandma's house for the day. We wouldn't get back to grandma's until like 10.30. It would be the same routine everyday inside and out. I would go straight into the lounge where my duvet would be there waiting. I would have to go and sit on the sofa with the blanket over me to make sure I didn't get cold. The fire would also be on full blast. It was boring towards the end (when I had put on some weight) but in the first few months of being there I really didn't care about being there, not because I liked it but because I just didn't want to live and didn't care what happened. My grandma and granddad basically stopped their lives too. One of them would be with me the whole day to make sure I didn't exercise or hide my food. I just sat in the chair watching TV and drawing. The first few weeks I wouldn't do anything until they said "Are you going to do anything today?" I would just sit in the chair staring into space. I think this was more to do with the fact that I hated everyone for putting me where I was and basically stopping me from doing what I wanted to do, which was lose more weight.

I would put my feet and arms out of the duvet in the effort to lose more weight. I would also move my legs loads under the covers as my bit of extra exercise. No one noticed this so I carried on doing it for most of the day in an attempt to lose weight. At every point when i was alone I would try to exercise. I had less than a week to lose weight before I was weighed. I didn't want to go to hospital but I really wanted to lose weight, so I would exercise under the covers and try to get cold more than trying to stop myself. This had totally taken over my life and head.

At lunchtimes I would eat in the chair where I had been all day. Grandma and granddad would eat theirs there too so they could watch me. It would take me so long to eat, probably about two hours. I would try everything I could think of to try to get out of eating it. For instance I would say things like "I'm too hot, I'm too cold, I'm too full up, I've got tummy ache, I'll eat it in a minute, can I have something else, I don't like this, I don't want this, I feel sick". None of these comments made any difference because grandma said she wasn't going anywhere until I had eaten it. I would sit there staring at the food just wanting to scream and throw it all on the floor. It sometimes took me so long to even start eating that grandma actually took the spoon of food and put in up to my face herself. This made me so angry when she did this because I just wanted to tell her to fuck off and run out the house and just keep running. I think the reason why I didn't do any of the things I wanted to was because I felt so low and too down to do anything and because deep down I knew I loved them. I hated what my anorexia was doing to me, it was making me hate everyone and I couldn't stop it. I believed everything it said to me. When I did finally start the food I would eat the smallest amounts with every spoonful. I was still trying to hide some of the food too by squashing it into the plate to make it disappear, hiding some food under the knife and fork, making loads of crumbs down either me or on the plate to make me have less calories, spreading food around the plate to make it look like it had gone or make a really big mess and leave some food rubbed into my hands for me to then have to go and wash my hands which was actually washing away the food. I don't think I ever finished a meal completely. I would always leave something because it made me feel so much better because I knew that I wasn't eating every calorie, so it meant I wasn't going to put on as much weight. My morning and afternoon snacks were generally chocolate bars, as you saw from the meals plans. This was an easy thing to get away with not eating it all so I managed to hide my snacks a lot of the time. I would take some of it out of the wrapper and hold it in my hand whilst eating another bit of it and then put the bit that was in my hand in my pocket. I would then get rid of the chocolate that was in my pocket by going to the toilet and wrapping it in tissue so it wouldn't melt. I would then place it in my bag. Each day when I came home from grandma's I would have to get rid of the food from my bag secretly. I placed it all in plastic bags around my bedroom. Mum had stopped searching my room by this time because she knew I was being watched 24/7 so there was no need for her to worry, but what she didn't know was that I was actually getting away with not eating everything. This made my anorexia happy and pleased with me so it put me in a better mood.

Each and every day the same thoughts would go around my head. I would do and say the same things each day to try and avoid eating and I would carry on doing my secret exercise. I was so motivated to do the exercise and try to not eat that I just had to do it. It became part of a routine that I couldn't let go of. I was so isolated and just wanted to spend my days doing nothing, apart from thinking about food and weight.

The week went past and my next appointment with Kirsti came. I was so scared about the meeting. I really didn't want to have put on weight; I did think I had put on weight though because I felt extremely fat and disgusting. Grandma took me and we met mum there. When Kirsti came out and called us in it was so awkward. Kirsti asked me how I was but I didn't really talk. I really didn't want anyone to know how I felt and I was just generally frustrated with everything and everyone. Kirsti had bought along Sue who was the nurse from the hospital I would be sent to. She thought it would be nice for us to meet each other and get to know each other because she thought it might help me realise what hospital was like. We talked a little but Sue did most the talking about how the hospital would be and she said that I was very lucky that CAMHS and my family agreed for me to stay at grandma's house because she thought I should have been in hospital from hearing what she had heard about my weight and from what I looked like. It was then the time I had been dreading, weigh time. I got weighed outside the room because I didn't want everyone seeing and watching. I had put on over 1KG and now weighed 36.9kg. I felt disgusting and immediately started thinking of how to lose it. When we entered the room Kirsti told everyone that I had gained weight. This meant I wouldn't have to go into hospital but it would be closely monitored and if I lost more weight I would still go into hospital. By then I think in a way I wanted to go to hospital because I felt that I would be able to fight them more because I wouldn't care if I swore at them because I didn't care about them the same way as I did about my family. I never really thought that if I was in hospital I wouldn't get to see my family each day and that it wouldn't be a nice place to be, all I thought about was losing weight and this was another possible way that I thought would help me to lose weight.

The next appointment was for a week's time and we arranged for Sue to come along to the meetings every six weeks so she could keep an eye on me as well. I was still not allowed to do anything and had to stay under the covers all day every day. I was really not happy. I tried everything I could to get out of eating.

The weekends were the best for me because I used to get away with hiding my breakfast as well as the snacks. Mum used to bring up my breakfast at about 8.30-9.00am and she used to go back into her room to read. She would keep coming to check on me but what she didn't know was that I wasn't actually eating what had disappeared from the plate, I was hiding it. I stored loads of plastic bags in my room and used to get out of bed and throw some of it in the bags and would eat a little bit so then when mum came in it looked as though I was eating it. I would then hide the bag behind my futon or under my covers. My anorexia was so happy and kept complimenting me on what I had done. I really hated lying to my mum because I knew she really thought I was doing well and she thought I was eating. She always said well done for eating it and was so encouraging and all I was doing was deceiving her and being nasty. I felt soooo bad and horrible about doing it, but obviously not bad enough to be able to stop myself. Once I had finished my breakfast my life would be the same as it was during the week. This was sitting around doing nothing. I wasn't even allowed to help put the decorations up on the weekend that we did it (Christmas 2008). I was so upset about that because I have always loved putting the decorations up and I was always so excited about Christmas like three months before the big day. Except this year was different. I couldn't even enjoy the Christmas music because I wasn't allowed to move or exercise one little bit. I did try and move my legs a bit but mum kept spotting me and telling me off.

The night of the pantomime came. I was really looking forward to it because it got me out of the house, it meant I was doing more exercise than I was allowed and it meant I would be able to get cold. All I was constantly thinking about was losing weight. I was never actually looking forward to the things we had planned. That morning I did my usual exercise while getting dressed. It was a really down day for me so anorexia punished me and made me do way over half an hour of jogging. Grandma started to suspect something was going on because I had taken much longer than normal so she came upstairs. She was standing outside my room for ages before she knocked. When she finally knocked I was naked (because I always had to watch myself in the mirror) so I said hang on while I quickly put my clothes on. She came in and looked angry. I didn't know what to say so I just stood there staring at her. She started talking to me about what I was doing and why I was doing it, but I couldn't handle all the questions and I also felt so bad and angry that she had caught me that I just started crying. I constantly felt drained and tired, but nothing stopped me from exercising. While I finished getting ready she stayed upstairs to watch me.

After that day was over when mum came to pick me up grandma told her that she had caught me exercising. Mum was really angry and started saying you don't want to go to hospital do you and why are you doing this, can't you see you're upsetting everyone. She didn't mean this horribly, she was trying to get through to me but couldn't because I wasn't listening to any of it. I was really angry with myself for letting grandma catch me out because I knew this would mean everyone would be on my case even more than they were already! I was also annoyed with grandma for telling mum. I thought she might have forgotten. I changed the subject by asking mum whether I could have a shower when we got in and grandma said "I don't know because you have done too much exercise already today and I don't think you should come out tonight either". I was getting so angry with grandma for even saying this, I wasn't even asking or talking to her anyway so I don't know why she even answered, and she was only saying this to scare me into eating, but this was just making it worse and worse and was making me hate her even more each day. Mum luckily said "well she has to shower" so luckily I managed to have a shower. I did go out to the pantomime in the end too because I ate my dinner without making a big fuss and without taking too long. Anorexia allowed me to not make a fuss this once because it knew I would be getting rid of it by going out later on. We went to see Scrooge in the local library. I can't remember what it was like to be honest and I think I switched off throughout part of it because I had so many other things going around in my head.

I think everyone thought that punishing me or saying bad things about the anorexia was going to help me fight it but what they didn't know was that it was making it even harder for me to cope with because I was already angry with the anorexia anyway, so that it then made me not like them. I couldn't tell mum that I didn't like it when they all said horrible things because she would say that she was too scared and didn't want to lose me, but the thing was it was making it harder. She didn't seem to recognise this though. This always makes me upset now, looking back on it; also the thought that I actually did hate mum and grandma for what they were doing to me. Now that I'm nearly recovered I'm so glad they were there and that I still have them in my life now.

I remember this one time when I refused to eat my lunch one weekday at grandma's so that she took away everything so I had nothing to do for the rest of the day. She thought that this would help me and make me eat because she thought I would get bored, but it didn't help. I didn't eat anything for the rest of the day because I was annoyed with her for punishing me for not eating so that I had to carry on and not let her see me getting upset. For the rest of the day I just sat there watching a bit of TV and staring into space. Anorexia wouldn't allow anyone else to win, apart from it.

I was still emailing my Aunty. I would write down how I was feeling and what I was getting annoyed about each time I wrote to her. This made me feel a bit better about life by getting the anger out of me and sharing it with someone else. Here are a few emails from me to her and from her to me about mum getting angry with me and how I was feeling.

Dear Jess,

Firstly I want to say how touched I am that you are talking to me. Secondly let me ask you a question. Where do you see yourself in 5 years? What would you like to do? Mum gets angry because she's scared. She loves you so much; we all do. She nearly lost you when you were born so premature and I expect a lot of those feelings are re awakening. It's good you understand why she got angry. Contrary to popular belief you don't know all the answers when you are an adult. So she is having to work hard to understand how you are feeling and why this is happening. As parents we always blame ourselves when things go wrong for our kids. So she is suffering too. I expect you have been told this loads but Jess, trust me, you are not even slightly overweight and never have been. You have your whole life ahead which is such a gift, something you get to realise when you are as old as me! That's why I asked you what you want to do; think about wishes you have, things you once thought you'd quite like to have a go at. Give yourself some other goals and things to aim for. Challenges faced can often make us feel stronger and feel better about ourselves. They don't have to be massive, just things that push us ever so slightly out of our comfort zone. So save the bungee jumping out of a helicopter for a few years!! (Your mother would kill me.)

Take care,

Love You

Mandy xx

This is one from me to my auntie.

Heya

That's OK. I am glad I can tell you all off this too cos it's someone new I can tell.

Um I dunno for sure what I want to be when I'm older. I would like to do something with art possibly but I haven't really thought about it.

Yeah I know I have a whole life ahead off of me. That's what everyone says. I do understand all of the things everyone tells me but I still can't believe it. Well I can, but the anorexia is stopping me from thinking and believing it.

I have joined this website called beat and I have been reading through some of the comments that the other people have written and it's all similar to how I'm feeling about myself etc.

Well I am on the recovery path but finding it hard. I am being made to eat 2500 calories a day and not allowed to exercise at all. I have to rest. I always have to be made to eat cos if I just got up and ate something myself without being told it will make me feel even worse than I do normally. This is because I will feel that I've given in to myself I think. I don't really know. Even though I want to get better I can't seem to want to at the same time. It's hard to explain.

It's hard to explain things too cos people just expect you to eat and be better but I don't think it's that easy. They say that anorexia is there for most of your life... it's soo bad. I used to weigh myself like 10 times a day and every time the numbers increased I immediately thought bad thoughts. When I weighed 6 stone I wanted to get down to 5 and a half, then when I was at that weight I wanted to get down to 5 stone. I just couldn't stop wanting to lose weight. I never got down to 5 stone and I feel kinda bad. Then when I got weighed at CAMHS last week and put on 3 pounds that now means I weigh 36.9 kilograms which I'm not that happy with. Well half of me is cos I didn't want to go into hospital and I want to get better but now I just feel even fatter and disgusting and I am still eating lots which is making it really hard. You probably don't understand any off this in the same way as me but oh well, I'll carry on. Mum has hidden the scales now so I don't no how much I weigh at all. I'm going to CAMHS to get weighed on Monday so I'll let you know how I've done. I dunno how I'm gonna feel if I put on more weight. I suppose it depends on how much. I'll let you know.

Every time I get upset or in a bad mood cos of how much I've eaten everyone just says well do you want to go to hospital and I say no so they say well you have to eat. It annoys me when people say do I want to go to hospital cos of course I don't but I don't think it's that easy to eat when your mind is telling you you can't and you're fat; you've already put on a lot of weight so you can't put on too much more etc. I don't believe that I'm thin but hopefully I will see it when I'm better.

I had some blood tests done yesterday and I now have a little lump and a bruise on my arm and mum said it's cos I have no fat on me but I don't see that. I don't see why nobody can see the fat on me cos I do. Well I had a slice of toast with chocolate spread and a bowl of crunchy nut clusters this morning plus my advent calendar. I'm having a mince pie too in half an hour. Grrrr. I hope I can eat it properly today and not feel too bad. For lunch I'm having a cheese and spinach cheesecake thing, a bread roll, a Muller yoghurt and some peanuts woo.

Then another snack, (a cereal bar) then steak tomatoes and potatoes for dinner with a pudding after. I would normally have another snack in the evening but I don't think I need one tonight mum said so I'm pleased about that.

I love you lots.

Hope you can understand some of this... sorry I babbled on...

Oh and I understand why everyone is making me eat. They're scared, I know. So hopefully this won't go on forever....

It's nearly Xmas.

How are you then?

Write back xxxxxxxx

Christmas 2008 came. I wasn't even that excited. I had nothing to look forwards to and all I was thinking about was the food. I am always excited about Christmas. It is the best time of the year in my opinion. On Christmas day we saw grandma and granddad and we played games and just had fun as a family. I wasn't that excited to spend Christmas with grandma and granddad because I was with them every day before Christmas so it wasn't as exciting and I knew that they would try and interfere with my food because they looked after me during the week so they also knew how big my portions should be and stuff. I did tell mum that this was something I was worried about and she said that she would talk to grandma and granddad about not saying anything to me or mum about what I was eating and she also said that she wasn't going to calorie count for Christmas day and boxing day, that she would allow me to put the veg on my plate because she wanted me to have the least possible stress. Once we had opened all our presents we got ready for some lunch. I was so nervous as usual. Mum dished up my turkey for me and she let me do everything else like she had promised. I didn't pick out a lot at all but to me it was enough and quite a lot. I knew I was going to find it hard and didn't want to feel worse for eating more than anorexia could handle so I listened to the anorexia once again. When Christmas day was over mum did get upset because she said that she thought I was taking advantage of her because I didn't take enough food and she said that I knew it wasn't enough so she didn't know why I didn't take more. I got upset by this too because I really thought I had done well and was pleased that I had even dished up my own food and I felt she was putting too much pressure on me, that she was wanting me to get better just like that. Mum did say sorry and we were all OK afterwards.

There was another programme on about anorexics in December 2008 and I decided to watch it this time to see whether any of the things they said or did were the same as what I was thinking and doing. It made me really upset because everyone on that programme was like a mirror of me. I didn't want to believe I was like them because I still didn't want to believe any of this was even happening. I didn't know what to do and just felt so alone. I was always so angry with myself and just hated myself so much.

In January 2009 I started self harming. I was finding it tougher than ever and just couldn't think about anything worse than living my worthless life. I had had another bad day at grandma's during the week where I had totally refused my whole lunch and my afternoon snack. This obviously made grandma and granddad upset and they were arguing a bit throughout the day. I knew this was because of me and I just thought I shouldn't be here because I was making everyone's life hell. I started drawing pictures in my sketch book that I had brought to grandmas of people that were thin. They weren't real people, just stick people but this helped make me like them and this then made me want to get even thinner and lose more weight to look like them. I would write down words like fat pig and I hate me to try to help me get my anger out but it didn't seem to help much, it just made me feel worse. I even wrote a note to mum in my notepad (I never gave it to her) that told her how I felt. I was so angry with myself and really wanted my life to end at this point. This is what the note said

To mum, I don't want to live with grandma and granddad any more. You're all being really horrible to me and you seem to think that I'm doing this on purpose; why? If I was doing this on purpose then surely before I was even diagnosed with anorexia I would have not been eating. I used to like having ice cream before I had anorexia so surely this isn't all me. You don't understand what I'm going through and you seem to think you do. You all keep saying you've got to eat that and this but it doesn't work like that. I'm finding eating really hard at the moment. Mum you said that if I don't try to get better then you want me to go somewhere else, well where do you want me to go? I've got nowhere else to go! And if you want me to leave so the family can be happy again why won't you let me die so I'll be out of you way then? You obviously don't want me to die so why do you keep saying you want me to leave when you won't let me.

I think I was finding eating even tougher than before because I felt really low. I was obviously depressed and I just felt that everyone was picking on me all the time and my family were always arguing about me so it made me feel really bad. Also mum, grandma and granddad kept saying the same old things over again to me because they were scared of losing me and they thought it would make me listen and be scared myself, but because I was so low and depressed I didn't really care any more about what happened and I knew I didn't want to live and that was that.

I was getting sent work home from college via emails every few weeks but I was finding it so hard to concentrate and focus on doing the projects. I really didn't care about my marks and just didn't want to spend any more of my time doing the work . I needed that time to finish counting up my calories for that day and figure out what I was having to eat next and how long I had left till the next dreaded meal time. It didn't help that every piece of work that I completed and sent back to my tutor came back with a fail or not up to standards. This then meant I had to restart it all and I was getting really upset. I had missed so much work that I soon decided that I wasn't going to do any more and that I was just going to focus on me instead of the college work.

One evening when I was upstairs I got my scissors and starting slitting my wrists and legs. I didn't really know what I was doing and why, to be honest. I just wanted the pain that I was experiencing to go away and just thought that this was the only solution. I never drew lots of blood but did draw a little. I felt happy that I was still in control, I felt this was like a new solution that every time I felt down I could cut myself to help me ease the pain. The self harming didn't last long though. Granddad was starting to get worried that I was depressed because most lunchtimes I was really quiet and wouldn't talk at all. He also suspected some other signs that I was showing that linked with depression so he called David and asked whether I could go and see him because he was worried about me. David said yes and made an appointment for the next day.

I was still hiding some of my snacks in my pockets and was still exercising every day in private. I had stopped exercising in the mornings while getting dressed because I was worried that grandma would find out again and I didn't want to risk getting anyone upset or worried about me again, so I had started exercising even later into the night than what I was already doing. I would jog in my room until like 1.00am. I was happy I was still able to do these things because it was helping me carry on with my life. Mum soon found out I was hiding my breakfasts from the weekends and some of my snacks because she suddenly had an outburst and suspected I might have been hiding food. I can't remember why she thought this, whether something went on for her to think this, but anyway she said she was going to look around my room for food and unluckily for me she found quite a bit of food. She was obviously very upset and annoyed once again with me and she really didn't understand why I was doing it. I was really annoyed with myself for letting her find it and anorexia was shouting at me, saying you're a silly cow, why didn't you hide it in a better place and stuff. I couldn't stop crying and kept saying I'm not doing this on purpose and that I was sorry.

Mum had also started to take her anger out on my anorexia in front of me so I just kept feeling it was me she was angry with because I couldn't see that I was ill. She said one thing, that was that she would let me eat anything I wanted if that's what I wanted and then when all my hair fell out again she would get everyone to laugh at me and see whether that made a difference. This was so hard for me to deal with and to hear her say these things to me, about anorexia. I know now definitely that she didn't mean it, she was so scared she didn't know what else to do.

Grandma and granddad sat me down one morning once I had arrived at their house and showed me this film on YouTube about anorexia and what affect it has on people. I just remember feeling really out of control, upset and angry by this point. I didn't like the fact that other people could see what anorexia was doing to me because I liked being the one with the control. I sat there and cried the whole way through it because they were all a mirror of how I was feeling and the way I was behaving over food. When it was over granddad spoke to me alone about why I was so upset. I wouldn't answer him and just stared at him blankly. He then opened up a word document for me to write down how I was feeling instead of me talking to him out loud. This didn't help me and I was still tensed up and didn't say anything at all. I couldn't let go of this grip anorexia had over me and I couldn't tell anyone how I was feeling. Anorexia was holding onto me with all its strength, but for some reason I liked it. I felt if I didn't have anorexia watching me like a hawk I'd lose all control of my life.

When the morning came I went to see David. Grandma and granddad came in the room with me so they could explain to David why they wanted me to see him. I didn't open up at all to David and hardly spoke to him. He seemed to be quite concerned for me too and said that he would put me on anti depressants. I can't really remember what my feelings were towards this. Grandma and granddad were then asked to leave the room so David could talk to me on his own. He asked me why they were worried about me and he asked me whether I had been self harming. I said that they were rightly upset and worried about me because I didn't enjoy talking or being with them, and I also said that I hadn't self harmed that much, which was a bit of a lie because I had been self harming for a few weeks before the appointment. The anti depressants were prescribed and I was to start them the next day after I got them. I had to take one a day. Earlier on before I was prescribed the medication I wrote on the website BEAT a message about how I really didn't want to live any more and how I wanted to die and stuff. They didn't even publish it on the message boards and instead wrote me an email saying that they were really worried and concerned about me because of some the things I had just written and that they thought I may have depression and suggested some other websites to go to for help. I didn't believe I had depression and didn't feel anything. I just wanted to die because I wanted my life to end.

Mum then found out that I had been self harming (I think from my Auntie) and she came into my room and took away everything I had in there that was sharp including my scissors, a few pens that were sharper than others and my compass because that had a sharp point on it.

By February/March time I was able to start doing a small amount, not full-on exercise but little things like walking around the town for a morning, or going shopping for a day with lots of breaks for me to rest. I didn't have to keep as warm as I had earlier on in the year and I was definitely feeling a little bit happier about this. The last few CAMHS appointments I had been to showed that I was putting on small amounts. I never knew what would happen every time I got on the scales because I kept losing and then putting small amounts on and vice versa. I still hated every moment of eating and also hated being weighed, especially when I had gained weight. The anti depressants were definitely working which was a good thing. The only thing that I was still finding hard was being around grandma and granddad's house all week every week, so mum came up with a plan. She would drop Mondays so I could stay with her on those days and then grandma and granddad could have a bit of their old life back, and on Fridays I would stay at home with my sister because that was her day off college. I felt a lot happier when this was put in place, especially because I felt like grandma and granddad were beginning to get annoyed with me always being there. I thought this because they were always arguing about who was going to go out on what day (because one of them had to stay with me) and where. They have always done a lot of group things like walking groups and holidays with friends and stuff which they had to stop in December 2008 and were now finding this hard to cope with and obviously wanted to start getting out and about again. I didn't mind them going out because I felt really bad about them not doing anything because it was entirely my fault. I was in their way, stopping their lives which I felt really bad about. I'm sure granddad didn't mean this to sound horrid but when he said it it made me feel really bad and upset about being there all the time. He got home from his walking group and grandma asked him how it was, what it was like and whether it was good, he said "Yeah I suppose but it would have been better if you were there." I told mum that I was starting to feel that they didn't want me there any more so that's why we all came up with the new routine. Mum did say that they didn't mean it at all and they were sorry if it upset me. I know now that they do love me and I'm really grateful for everything they've done for me.

During the next few weeks because I didn't have to stay as warm as I did before I was on the computer all day while I was at grandma's. I was constantly searching for things to help me lose weight like laxatives and diet pills. I was trying to find out as much information as I could about how I could lose weight and what I had to do. I never did order any, but this was only because I had no way of getting the stuff to my house without mum asking what it was or seeing it. This then made me feel annoyed that I was always being watched. I felt like a little child, not having any independence. It was horrible and it was everything anorexia disliked. This shows how much of a grip anorexia still had over me after being put on antidepressants and even after putting on a little bit of weight. It was so determined to not let me get better.

Kirsti had suggested to both mum and me that we should try out family therapy. I really wasn't interested in this and didn't want to go, but Kirtsi said it might help the whole family to deal with my anorexia and how to cope and get on with life, so we made an appointment with Emily who was the lady who ran the family therapy classes (the same lady I saw on my first ever appointment). We only went to two or three because none of us thought it was that good. In the family therapy sessions all we did was talk about me and how everyone as a family was coping with it all and why they thought it had happened. They had a microphone and cameras in the room where we were so that David and another member of the team could hear and see what we were doing. This was in case David and the team thought of something to say that was different from Emily, or if he thought something wasn't quite right, he would phone the room we were in and then talk. We would all be able to hear what David had to say too so it didn't make it feel awkward or anything. I just didn't like family therapy and preferred keeping myself to myself.

My appointments with Kirsti were still every week, but because I had put on some weight we actually started with the counselling. We would draw pictures and do questions and Kirsti wrote down notes on things I would say. She also gave me little tasks and activities to complete ready for the next appointment. These were all meant to help me open up and talk about what had happened to me and what I thought may have triggered the anorexia and various things like that. I feel the counselling helped me get my life back on track because if I hadn't had the help I might not be here now, but I didn't ever look forward to going. I only ever liked being weighed because I liked knowing what I weighed.

In March 2009 I decided to buy a frog. I had researched all about them and had written down everything I needed to know about how to handle and care for them. I was really excited about getting a frog because frogs are my favourite animal. I think this pet frog idea was a really good goal because it made me think about something else throughout the days instead of food all the time. I think this frog has also helped me to get better. After I had bought the tank and all the accessories the next weekend mum, my sister, my step dad and I went to this garden centre called Shoots. I looked around and picked out my frog. When I got him home I was so happy and couldn't stop watching him. He's called Pork and he's a Whites tree frog. He's lovely and I still adore him and also sometimes still can't believe I have a frog as a pet. Mum said I could only get a pet if I was going to live and if I wanted to live so this really helped me to make my decision on life. I decided I wanted to live and I really wanted a pet.

Chapter 9

Recovery

Life was getting better for me and the family. I was only seeing grandma and granddad three times a week, there were still arguments between mum and me about food and my weight and all the normal anorexia thoughts but in general I did feel happier. I had stopped hiding food, apart from the odd occasion when I really had to get out of eating. Unfortunately I was still up all night exercising, but wasn't losing loads of weight in one go so no one ever became suspicious. I was allowed to do things which made me happier and I wasn't treated so much as an inpatient. People were more relaxed around me. The anti depressants were like a life saver. If I hadn't had them, I would have still been slitting myself and one of those cuts could have been deadly and I would no longer be here right now.

We had planned to go away in August to Florida and I really really wanted to go so I knew I had to be better by then. I had started setting goals in my head about the future and I had started getting my old life back again. I had been seeing a few friends on the odd occasion to help me get back into a normal social life. When I was ill all I wanted to do was be on my own, I didn't want to see friends or go out, I just wanted to do exercise and think about food and calories.

Kirsti and mum had started asking me whether I was going to go back to college. They wanted to know what I wanted to do with my life because once I was able to go back to college they wanted me to be prepared for it and they wanted to be able to do a deal with the college for me to start off with three days a week or something to ease me back in gently and also so CAMHS could monitor my weight still. Every time this question was asked I would go into silent mode because I didn't like talking about college and I didn't really want to go back, but I was scared to say that. I had missed almost a year and had fallen behind so much that I didn't want to go back or talk about it. I think I found this hard to talk about because when I started at college, that was the year when I was ill and it spiralled out of control from then on quite quickly. I was hiding nearly all my food at lunch times and was hardly eating anything at college so I was worried about going back down that same route. I also said I didn't enjoy college but now thinking about it that might have been because I was so ill that I didn't like doing anything apart from exercise. I'm not too sure what the real reason is though.

A few weeks later I was thinking about what I could do with my life instead of going back to college. I had to find something else that I could do because I was adamant by then that I didn't want to go back to college. I had decided I didn't want to go to any other college either so the only solution was to find a job. I did research and found out that I could do an apprenticeship in childcare. I thought this a was good idea because I had always liked children and babies and did do lots of research on childcare while I was at school too, so this was obviously something I had wanted to do most of my life.

I then emailed lots of nurseries and phoned some and asked about any possible Trainee jobs. Some replied with application forms so I filled them out and sent them off. I then waited to see what would happen. Everyone was so pleased that I had come to a decision about what I wanted to do with my life and they were all pleased with what I had chosen to do.

The end of May was the deadline for the rest of the deposit to be paid for the holiday to Florida. This meant that we had to make a big decision on whether we were going to go in August or whether we were going to postpone it. I really wanted to go in August because I knew everyone was really looking forward to it too and I had already messed up and stopped all the family's life so I really wanted to go for their sake. I got really upset when everyone else said that they thought we should postpone it because it just felt as if they were saying that because they thought I wouldn't cope with it, which was nice of them of course but I didn't think that at the time. It felt as if I was letting them down again. Once mum had explained to me that we would rebook it for April 2010, when I would be even better and I would enjoy it so much more I felt happier about the decision. The thing was I really wanted to go on this holiday and didn't actually think we would be able to rebook it.

So when May time came we rebooked the holiday to Florida. I was so excited about going. The only thing that was playing on my mind was that I wouldn't be able to eat my food from my meal plan, I would have to eat out most days so we as a family decided to go out for a few meals before we went away so I could get used to it and to see how I felt about myself after eating out. This was a good plan and we ate out on a couple of occasions. They both went really well as far as I can remember. We sat in the more hidden seats in the restaurants and this made me find it a bit easier. I also felt more relaxed about the holiday to Florida because mum said that I would be able to eat salads as a meal because the portions over there are a lot bigger than England. I was really glad she had said that because this really reassured me about going and eating out in Florida. Salads are one of my safe foods so this reassured me for sure.

My 17th birthday came and I really didn't know what i wanted to do. I think this was also because I was more focussed on getting a job and sorting my life out. In the end I decided to get my nails painted in a salon with a couple of friends and to have them over to stay the night. It was a great day and I didn't get too nervous about eating in front of my friends, which was good. I had to show that I could do it as we wouldn't be going to Florida.

My eating was getting better, I was managing to eat everything that was put in front of me, but it would still take me an hour or so to eat it all. I still had the occasional blip but nothing major. I also still had really strong anorexic thoughts but all in all it was going fine and was under control. The most important thing that was keeping me going was the sudden urge to start my new life.

My CAMHS appointments were more spread apart by this time. Instead of going once a week I had started going every six weeks. In between those six weeks I weighed myself at home on the wii fit once a fortnight. This was much better and I liked it like this. I would still know how much I weighed and mum would know how many calories to plan for the week depending on my weight. I also liked seeing Kirsti less because I didn't feel much was happening towards the end. We would just talk like we were friends and we didn't really have many problems to talk about so it felt like the right thing to do.

Christmas 2009 was much better than 2008. I was happier, didn't think about food throughout the whole day and I was generally excited again about Christmas. I was allowed to put up the Christmas tree with the family and was allowed to do all the normal things normal people do. I could even dance to the Christmas music. Christmas 2009 was a happy and enjoyable one.

Chapter 10

Finding My New Life

A couple of weeks after filling out the application forms I had some replies saying that I had an interview. I was really excited to start my new life and career and couldn't actually believe this was happening.

Once the interviews were arranged I told everyone when they were for. I emailed my Auntie and told her. She was so pleased for me and she was so happy that I had come this far. Here are a few of the emails to her and from her.

Hi Jess,

Well done on getting not one but two interviews. That is fantastic. I am so proud of you. Please feel free to use me as a reference at any time. Had a lovely day today. It was sports day and it was great. The kids were brilliant and all cheered each other on. Did the third part of the swimming training this afternoon so spent the afternoon at the pool.

Have a brilliant birthday on Sunday.

Loads of love

Mandy xx

To Aunty Mandy

Another update ha-ha I got the job! I have a trial week on Monday and then if I enjoy it I can have the placement offered! This is a nursery in Hove; it the best one I thought and the one that I wanted! Omg I'll let you know how it all goes soon!! XXXX

Hi Jess,

Well done, darling. That is fantastic news. I am so proud of you. I bet you are so excited and especially to get the one you really wanted. You'll be fab. All well here. Went out for an Indian on Sunday night for Matt's birthday. It was really nice, then home for birthday candle in pile of choc brownies. The boys and I went strawberry picking in the morning so made heaps of strawberry jam. Matt got his hamster on Saturday; he is really pleased with her and has called her Syrup as she is Syrian and sweet. She is really cute, Cam calls her little dude and even Scottie is fascinated.

Take care

I got told I had the job at 11.00am on Monday 22nd June 2009. I was in Tesco with my mum doing the shopping at the time and I was awaiting the phone call because the nursery said they would call me on the Monday and let me know what was decided. When I got the phone call I was so delighted. I kept thinking the worst and was trying to prepare myself for not getting it, so I was over the moon when they said I could have the job. I started the trial week on the 29th June 2009. I wasn't nervous one bit. I think I was so eager for this that I had no worries. I just wanted to get started. On the 29th I got ready and headed out for my first day at work. I really enjoyed it. My basic duties were looking after the children and making sure they were OK and weren't in danger. At the end of the trial week the manager called me in the office to chat about how it had been and how I'd done. She said at first I wasn't very good but then towards the end of the week I was getting better and she could see the improvement. She said that my trial week was going to continue into next week and she would decide from then. I was happy with this and enjoyed every moment.

Over that week I got an email from grandma and granddad. They read as follows

Just heard from mum that you have got the job. Congratulations and a big hug from me -I just knew you could do it. I am so pleased for you and hope that you are very happy there. Look forward to seeing you over the weekend -I've missed my mate around the house.

Love Granddad

Hey Jess

Is it true what I heard from Mum, that you have got the job? You must have done your absolute best as you texted you would to me yesterday. I am so proud of you, you have really done very well indeed.

I look forward to hearing all about Jim and the other babies and children on Saturday when we are at Party in the Park.

CONGRATULATIONS - YOU DESERVED TO GET THE JOB AND NOW YOU CAN SHOW THEM HOW QUICKLY YOU CAN LEARN EVERYTHING YOU HAVE TO.

Look forward to seeing you on Saturday.

All my love

Grandma

XXXXXXXXXXXXXXXXXXXXXXXXXXXXXXXXXXXXX XXXXXXXXXXXXXXXXXXXXXXXX

Hi Jess, Hope your week has gone well -you should be getting into the groove now-only another 50 years before retirement. Hope you have not been bitten, slapped or pooed on and all the babies are getting used to you. Just attaching something that you might like to do for old times' sake.

Lots of love Granddad XXX

The thing that he attached was some mandali puzzles. We used to do them every lunchtime once I had started getting better, so from about March to June.

Grandma and granddad have been so lovely. They have looked after me and played a huge part in my life with getting me better. They were the ones who stopped me from going into hospital and they were the ones who helped me get this job because they drove me to the interviews and were so supportive the whole way. Shame I didn't see this at the beginning.

Once the trial week was over with the manager offered me the job. I was so pleased and happy and couldn't wait to tell everyone. The only thing was, I didn't know what was going to happen in a couple of months' time. In September she called me into her office and said that I wasn't doing very well and that I wasn't socialising with the children and she thought I was vacant. I asked her what I had to do to be more sociable with the children because I thought I was doing really well but she didn't really give me any advice on this matter. She said if she had to talk to me again then she would have to consider getting rid of me. (Words to that effect anyway). I was sociable with her and she never really seemed to talk back to me. I kept asking her questions about my training and when it would get started and she just said she didn't really know and I'd have to wait and see. She says she did tell me that I had to wait six months before the training started but I know she didn't say this as I wouldn't have kept asking her. I used to ask her how she thought I was doing and about my progress and stuff and she never said anything bad. I thought everything was going well but then in October I was called into the office again. She said that basically I hadn't improved over the time that she had last spoken to me, she said that I was a liability to the children (I didn't know what this meant until I told mum and she said it means you're a danger) she said that I was always vacant whenever she saw me and that I wasn't interacting with the babies. I asked her lots of questions on how I was meant to interact with the babies and I said to her something like "I talk to them all the time and cuddle them and play with them, how else I am meant to interact with them especially if they can't talk back or do things back with me?" She didn't really ever answer these questions. I also said "How am I meant to improve when I haven't even started my training and you're saying I'm not doing well but everyone else is saying I'm doing really well?" Someone was lying. She finally said that I could no longer work at that nursery but there was a position at the Dyke Road nursery if I wanted that job. She said that if I didn't take that offer I basically wouldn't have a job. I said I would think about it and let her know the next day. That evening I told mum all about the meeting and I got really upset. Mum was really angry with my manager for treating me like that and she phoned them up and said that she wanted a meeting with the manager and me so she could discuss this further. The nursery agreed to this, so the next working day went by and in the evening we went to the staff room for the meeting. They basically said the same things to mum as they had to me so I said I would like the other job.

The next day I went home early so I could have a look around the new nursery. It looked really nice and the people seemed nice which was good. I then started at that nursery on the Monday. I'm still here now doing my training for my level 2 in childcare. I'm really pleased I got moved over because I get on so much better over at Dyke road. I hated the other manager after what she'd said to me and will never forgive her for what she did and how she treated me during those couple of months when I had been working there.

While this was all going on I had saved enough money to start driving lessons. I had always wanted to drive and was desperate to start learning and to eventually get my own car. I started learning on the first weekend in October 2009. I had a really nice instructor and we got on well so that was good. My instructor said I was doing really well with the driving. I booked my theory test soon after and it was booked for 14th November 2009. I did revision for it most nights up until the exam. I passed it first time and was really happy. This meant I could book my driving test which I knew I could do soon because my instructor had said that he thought I was ready for it. So I then booked my test the day after my theory for January 2010. Unfortunately I failed this one so booked it again. My second one was booked for the 17th March 2010 and I passed this one. I was over the moon and was so happy. I had already bought my car in January so this meant I could drive straight away. I bought a ford fiesta from a small car garage near my house. On the day of my second test after I'd passed I decided to go for a drive in my new car so I went to the Crawley shopping mall and did a bit of shopping. It was great to have my own freedom and to be able to drive around wherever and whenever I wanted. I now drive to work every day instead of getting the train.

By this time my eating was so much better. I still stuck with everything on the meal plans and didn't eat anything extra because I was still really scared about eating anything that wasn't planned. My exercise was better though. I wasn't exercising anywhere near as much as I had been before I started the job. I think this was partly because I was so tired from my days at work and just didn't think about it as much because I had other things on my mind. I was so much happier at my new work (Dyke Road). Everyone there is so much nicer and seems to like me more so it's made me enjoy it loads more. Now I know that I have definitely got a career ahead of me because I've almost finished my training. My motivations are working to gain my level 2, my car and my family.

Mum had also said when I was ill that when I was better she would take me to see Rihanna in concert because I had really always wanted to see her, but because I was too ill I couldn't go if she went on tour so this was a thing to try and make me get better. Luckily she went on tour in 2010 and mum stuck to her promise and took me to see her. She was fabulous and I loved it.

When I went to CAMHS for my February appointment 2010 we discussed being taken off the anti depressants because I felt so much better and everyone else felt that I had changed and were happy for this to happen. After this discussion we decided to go for it and I was then taken off the anti depressants the next week. I was happy with this decision but was a bit nervous at the same time because I was worried I might get really low again. I was worried that the only reason I was happy and more into life was because of the anti depressants. This wasn't true though because since I have been off them I haven't been put back on them.

Chapter 11

Holiday To Florida

April 2010

The holiday that we had been waiting for since the year before had finally come. We were all very excited about this and couldn't believe we were actually going this time. I was extremely happy because I wanted to go the year before but I didn't want to upset anyone or make everyone feel that I was the only one stopping them from going. Now looking back I'm really glad we did decide to go in April instead of August because I was so much better. Just that little amount of time I had changed loads. I was like a different person.

We jetted off on the 2nd April and went for two weeks. It was great out there. It was the best holiday I had been on. I really enjoyed it. I didn't even get too worried about the food either. I had Caesar salads most lunchtimes but then for dinner I had a normal meal. I did make sure though that I chose the smallest amounts of food from the buffets because I was still worried about putting on weight. I was happy about the exercise part of it though because we walked around the theme parks all day so I knew I was getting enough exercise. I was really glad I didn't think about food and exercise much because it made me really enjoy the holiday.

While we were away we went to all the big theme parks including sea world, typhoon lagoon, wet and wild, universal studios, animal kingdom, magic kingdom, islands of adventures, Epcot and Hollywood studios. I loved them all and enjoyed every moment.

When the holiday was due to come to an end we couldn't get home for another week because an earthquake had erupted. We were moved into another hotel that was closer to the airport. I was starting to worry by this point because it would be over three weeks since I was last weighed and I was really worried I had put on weight. I had no idea what had happened with my weight because I hadn't weighed myself. Luckily there was a swimming pool at this hotel so I managed to go in there for an hour most days. This made me feel a bit better about not being able to weigh myself.

When we finally got home a week after our due date I weighed myself to see how I was doing. I had lost a few pounds which made me feel good about myself, especially because I thought I would have put on weight because I had been on holiday. I'm glad I lost weight because I find it more scary putting on loads of weight in one weighing then losing loads.

Chapter 12

My 18th Birthday

The day of my 18th birthday finally arrived. I was so excited about being eighteen because I couldn't wait to go out to the pubs and order my own drink and just generally have alcohol legally. On my actual birthday, 7th June, I went out to the pub down my road with a few friends. I had red wine. It was a really good night. We only had the chance to have a couple of drinks each because I had work the next day and mum and my step dad had work as well.

The thing I was really looking forward to was the weekend after. I was having a party in the local pub down town. We had a disco too and everyone enjoyed themselves. It was such a good night. That was the first time I had ever actually got drunk. It felt so good to be able to drink whatever, whenever. My birthday was a success and I was happy.

The only thing I was worried about was the drink because alcohol has loads of calories in it and I was just worried that I would start to put on weight more quickly because I would be eating way over 2000 calories. Luckily this thought didn't ruin my evening.

Now that I'm eighteen I go out all the time to the pubs and out clubbing and I am not that worried about the calories. When I'm drinking I don't think about it at all, but in the following days I then do some exercise just to make me feel better about myself.

I sometimes think that I'm going too much the other way now, like when I drink alcohol I seem to like to drink loads. I have calmed down now because everyone gets worried when I drink too much, obviously because it's not good for your insides. I have already had a couple of times when I have been sick and got too drunk to remember the night so I have really thought this through and am just reminding myself that this time last year I would never have wanted to drink alcohol so I really need to control myself because I don't want anything to happen to me through drink. That really wouldn't be good. I've had two really bad years with food, so can't now have two bad years with drink. I think maybe this was just a phase because I never drank before I was eighteen really, so it's like a dog being let of the lead. It's a new experience, but I'm not going to let it get too out of control because I want to live my life from now on.

I got money from my step mum this year. She wrote in the card

To Jessica

From (her name)

This was really strange because it didn't come from dad, so I don't know whether he knew about this or not. When I wrote the thank you letter I just wrote it to my step mum. I didn't even get a happy birthday text from my dad this year either, even on a big number birthday!. At least my step mum is trying to be normal with me. I still haven't received a text from my dad saying happy birthday. I don't let this upset me now because I think it's all just childish games and no one's achieving anything by acting this way.

Chapter 13

Nearly Recovered

Well I have been discharged from CAMHS since July 2010. I was happy about being discharged because it meant i was almost better and it meant that I didn't have to miss any more work by going to the appointments. I had to be discharged from CAMHS because I was eighteen. I had the choice of being referred to adult services but I didn't want to because I thought I'd be OK and I wanted to start my new life afresh. I also didn't think they would help much because I wasn't finding CAMHS much help towards the end.

Since July to the present I am doing really well. I go out drinking a lot and don't really think about anything, definitely nowhere near as much as I used to anyway. I do still have the odd days where I hate myself, but not to the extreme of not wanting to live any more.

I only do about thirty minutes of exercise every time I do exercise because mum doesn't want me to do too much at once because that's not normal. I would probably do more at one time if I was allowed to.

I don't think I'll ever know what triggered my anorexia and I don't even know whether I want to know. I also don't think my anorexia will ever be fully cured because I do still worry when I put on weight and still want to lose weight when I put it on. My anorexia thoughts are bearable and I'm happy with that. I think if I didn't have any anorexic thoughts I would be worried because I have had them for so long now that it feels like security. It helps me get on with my life, So I'm glad I still think this way and am also glad that I never did die.

My relationship with my family is back to the old ways now which is really nice; I never thought I would get here.

Chapter 14

The End

This is the end of my story. I am really pleased I have come this far and am hoping for it to stay this way. I don't think the anorexia will ever completely disappear from my life so I now have a life that is constantly being controlled by anorexia. Hopefully not bad though, I mean I can still do things, I will just have to change my food that I eat on the days I'm out and the days I'm not.

Just a quick note before I go, to all you anorexics out there: I know you can do this, just keep fighting, and if I managed to do it then you all can. Don't give up and try to think of the things you want to do in life as this may help you because once I found out that I had some objectives to aim for I slowly started getting better.

To all the people out there who feel they are getting signs of anorexia: however much you want to lose weight, please try not to get into this state, it's not a good place to be and I can promise you that it's a really really hard recovery. Please try not to get like this and don't ever stop eating or over exercise as part of a deal because before you know it you will be out of control and anorexia will be starting to take over your life. Make sure you talk to your friends and family about how you're feeling so they can help you too and get professional help.

To all the parents out there who think their child is getting anorexia: join BEAT and leave comments on there to get advice on what to do. Don't be afraid to get professional help if you can and make sure you ask your child what they are feeling and how they are in themselves; don't let them slip away in their own world if you can. Even though they won't want your help, don't give up because like me, I got the help but didn't want it and look at me now!. Also get them interested into something they really want, e.g. a new pet (like my pet frog) because this is a really good incentive to aim for with getting better.

To mum and family and to everyone who has helped me: thank you so very much for everything you have done. I don't know what I would have done without you lot. I probably wouldn't be here. I really don't know how I'm ever going to be able to show you how much I love you all and I'm really sorry for putting you through the last few years of hell.

Love you all! Xx

Anorexia is not an attention seeking thing like many people think, it's a serious illness that has to be recognised before it's too late. It's not just about how little you eat or how much you exercise, it's a life threatening illness that affects the mind. It is a mental illness that could kill you, so if anyone has someone they know that is suffering don't let them suffer alone, help them out and get them professional help instead of befriending them and leaving them isolated and alone.

What is anorexia? Anorexia is a life threatening illness that takes over your mind, and controls your every move. You think it's your friend but all it's trying to do is tear you apart from your friends and family. You trust anorexia and believe every little thing it tells you and you don't believe what the real people tell you. When you receive help anorexia doesn't like it and tries to get you to lie and pretend that you're eating. It shows you a distorted vision of your body image which makes you believe that you're fat when a lot of the time you're thin.

It has a big grip on you and does everything it can to keep that control over you and to make you listen to it. It punishes you if you disobey it or do something it doesn't like. My punishments anorexia made me do were exercising loads, hiding food and lying. Anorexics have an intense fear of gaining weight so they do everything they can to get out of eating. This is a nasty disease and everyone should feel able to get professional help when needed.

How does anorexia affect your body? Anorexia makes you constantly feel drained and tired. You're always aching and you can never get comfortable. You always feel like you need to be on the move. Anorexia stops your menstrual cycle, leaving you with a high percentage of not being able to have children when you're older, leaves your skin looking pale and shapeless, leaves your hair and nails brittle, gives you a high chance of having osteoporosis (brittle bones).